Beneath the Thistle Sky

Written by
Vicky Donald

Copyright

The moral rights of the author have been asserted

All rights reserved

No part of this publication maybe reproduced, stored in a retrieval system or transmitted in any form or by any means, without the prior permission in writing of the publisher or the author, nor be otherwise circulated in any form of binding or cover other than that in which it is published and without a similar condition including this condition being imposed on the subsequent purchaser.

Name : **Parker Publishers**

Address: **UK: 71-75 Shelton Street,**
Covent Garden, London, WC2H 9JQ

www.parkerpublishers.co.uk

Our books may be purchased in bulk
for promotional, educational, or business use.
Please contact **Parker Publishers**
at **020 4579 4589**, or by email at
info@parkerpublishers.co.uk

First Edition 2025

Ebook: 978-1-918199-09-3
Paperback: 978-1-918199-10-9
Hardback: 978-1-918199-11-6

Dedication

This book is dedicated to my family, who are now and will always be my inspiration for so many of my poems.
For those who are no longer with us, I thank you for all the wisdom you passed to me that I now pass on to my own four beautiful daughters. I miss you all more than any words I could ever write.

To all my beautiful siblings, I love you all and thank you for the inspiration you have given me from childhood fights to our very grown, very proper nights out!
To my parents, thank you for everything and for always believing in me. I love you both very much.

To my husband Gary, you are my soulmate and give me so much inspiration always. You are now and will always be the only person who can make me laugh, no matter the situation!

To my daughters and my biggest inspiration, you are all beautiful both inside and out. You make me prouder every day. Always be who you are and never let anyone tell you that you cannot achieve your dreams.

Finally, to an incredibly special friend, Chloe, you always pushed when I needed it and for that, I thank you so very much.

Vix xx

Foreword

This book of poetry has been a lifelong pursuit that has finally come to life.

I have written poetry for many years. I was once told that when I was mad or sad or feeling overwhelmed to pick up a pen and just write. No matter what comes out, just write, throw away the paper and then you will feel better. Well, for me what eventually came out was poetry. I am so grateful for that advice because without it, my poetry may never exist.

This book is a mix of my poetry from over the last 3 years. From Politics in Scotland to just everyday life, with some Scots poems too.

I hope you enjoy and maybe even relate to some too.
Thank you.

Acknowledgements

My deepest gratitude goes to my publishers and proofreader — thank you for your care, patience, and belief in my work. Your guidance helped bring these words to life just as I imagined them.

To my S4 English teacher, Mr. Boyd — thank you for reigniting my passion for writing at a time when I had almost forgotten it. Your encouragement reminded me that words have power, and that my voice was worth sharing. Here's the book you swore you would see one day!

To my Grandad, who first sparked and nurtured my love for reading and writing — every poem I create carries a little of what you taught me. Your influence will forever live between the lines.

To my readers — thank you for opening your hearts to my words. Your support gives meaning to every page.

And to my friends & family, who have spent years encouraging me to finally write this book — your faith in me kept this dream alive. I'm forever grateful for your love, laughter, and belief.

With love and gratitude,
Vix

POLITICAL POEMS

LET DOWN

In Fife streets, where sun shines bright and bold,
A story unfolds, of a heart so young and bold.
My 18-year-old daughter, with abilities astray,
A learning disability, a label to stay.

Does it define her worth? Does it tell her fate?
Is she less deserving of love, of hope, of state?
No, my child, your worthy, just like everyone else born,
Your spirit beats strong, your dreams yet to be sworn.

The school door close, and a void appears in sight.
No job, No help, just a lonely, endless night.
Fife Council's silence, a deafening sound,
The Scottish Government's promises, lost, without a bound.

Why do they turn a blind eye? Why do they ignore?
Leaving you, dear one, with just me and more?
Mum and Dad, your guiding lights, your safe haven too,
But shouldn't there be more, for a young life anew?

We search for answers, for solutions, for a way,
To bridge the gap, to seize each passing day.
For a future bright, for a life full and wide,
Not just for some, but for you, side by side.

So let us rise, let our voices be heard,
Demanding change for those who've been blurred.
Let Fife Council, let Scotland take a stand,
And provide for all, a helping hand
Our daughter, eighteen, with a heart so true,
Deserves a chance, to live, to grow anew.
She's not defined by her limitations alone,
Her spirit, her smile, make her worthy, her own.

So let us fight, for a brighter tomorrow,
For inclusion, equality, for every single hour.
For our own daughter, for others like her too,
A life of dignity, a life anew.

THISTLE & STEEL

The heather weeps, a purple bruise,
Across the glens, the chilling news.
No bagpipes drone a mournful sound,
But sirens wail on hallowed ground.
A thistle bleeds, its prickling crown,
As innocence is stricken down.

Young eyes, once bright with highland fire,
Now gleam with something dark and dire.
The steel they flash, a twisted boast,
A stolen childhood dearly lost.

Each shadowed lane, a whispered fear,
Of blades that gleam and futures near,
Consumed by rage, a hollow pride,
Where youthful dreams have gone to hide.
Parents clutch, with hearts ablaze,
Afraid to lose in this iron maze.

The ancient stones, they stand and stare,
At broken vows and whispered prayer.

Can Scotland rise, her spirit mend,
And teach these children how to bend,
The steel they craft, the hands to heal,
And learn the wounds are truly real?
To trade the blade for open hand,
And reclaim peace within the land.

A SHADOW OVER SCOTLAND

A shadow falls on Scotland's youth,
A darkness bred of rage and ruth,
Girls on girls, a brutal scene,
A vicious fight, both fierce and mean.

Girls on boys, a power play,
Leaving victims in dismay.
Boys on boys, a hateful clash,
A violent storm, a bitter clash.

The blows are dealt, the damage done,
Yet justice sleeps beneath the sun.
No punishment, no hand to stay,
The violence grows with each new day.

The government, a silent watch,
Ignoring cries along the path.
The police their hands are tied,
A helpless force, they cannot hide.

The anger festers, deep and sore,
A poison spreading more and more.
A cycle spins, a grim despair,
A future lost, beyond repair.

The streets echo with silent screams,
A broken land, it sadly seems.
Where youth turn cruel, and hope takes flight,
Lost in the shadows of the night.

A FREE SCOTLAND

In the hills where the thistle's sway,
The spirit of Scotland forever will play,
With the Saltire flying high and proud,
Beneath its embrace, we gather a crowd.

Tartan patterns weave tales of old,
Of battles fought and warriors bold,
With William Wallace, a name that inspires,
Kindling the heart of freedom's fires.

The winds whisper stories of blood and pride,
Of those who stood tall and never would hide,
In the shadows of heather, with courage they bled,
For a land of their own, where dreams could be fed.

In valleys and glens, the echoes still call,
To rise up for justice, for once and for all,
With hearts intertwined, let our voice proclaim,
For Scotland, our home, we will honour her name.

So let the Saltire wave in the sky,
And the spirit of freedom forever soars high,
As we tread on this land, with courage anew,
To honour our past and embrace the true blue.

A LETTER FROM THE BUNKER

I do not sleep; I count the cost -
Of every inch of ground, we've lost.

The sirens wail, the children cry,
And still, beneath a wounded sky,
I lead with hope, though hope runs thin -
This war, we must not let win.

Across the sea, a voice resounds,
Not to defend, but to confound.

Trump speaks not peace, nor warns the foe,
But mocks the pain he'll never know.

He praises might, not human right,
And leaves us stranded in the night.

He bullies from his golden tower,
As if this fight were just for power.

But here we bleed, and here we stay,
We fight for dawn, for light, for day.

I may be small, my army lean,
But truth stands tall where lies have been.

So let him jeer, and let him scorn,
This land is mine – I am Ukraine-born.

And when this war has passed us by,
And all the smoke has left the sky,
The world will ask: who stood, who ran?

Who stood for peace, and who for man?

FROM THE HIGHLANDS WATCHING

I am the land of mist and stone,
Where ancient winds have always blown.
From crag and glen, I watch the strife -
The shattering of home and life.

Ukraine fights fierce, her banner high,
While fire rains down from a tainted sky.
And I, a nation forged by fight,
Know what it means to guard the right.

But strange it is, across the sea,
To watch the land once proud and free,
Embrace a tyrant's poisoned charm,
And praise the hand that deals the harm.

Trump, who talks of strength and deals,
Knows not the weight a soldier feels.
He lifts no arms, but tweets with glee,
While freedom drowns across the sea.

And Zelensky – bold, a poet's flame -
Stands in the smoke and speaks his name.
He bears the world upon his brow,
While coward clamour, shouting "how"?

I've held my pride through battles grim,
But ache for those with hope grown dim.
For though I lie in peaceful moor,
The call of justice shakes my shore.

Let nations rise, not turn away,
From those who die for light of day.
For history sees, and truth will tell -
Who let the strong give war its spell.

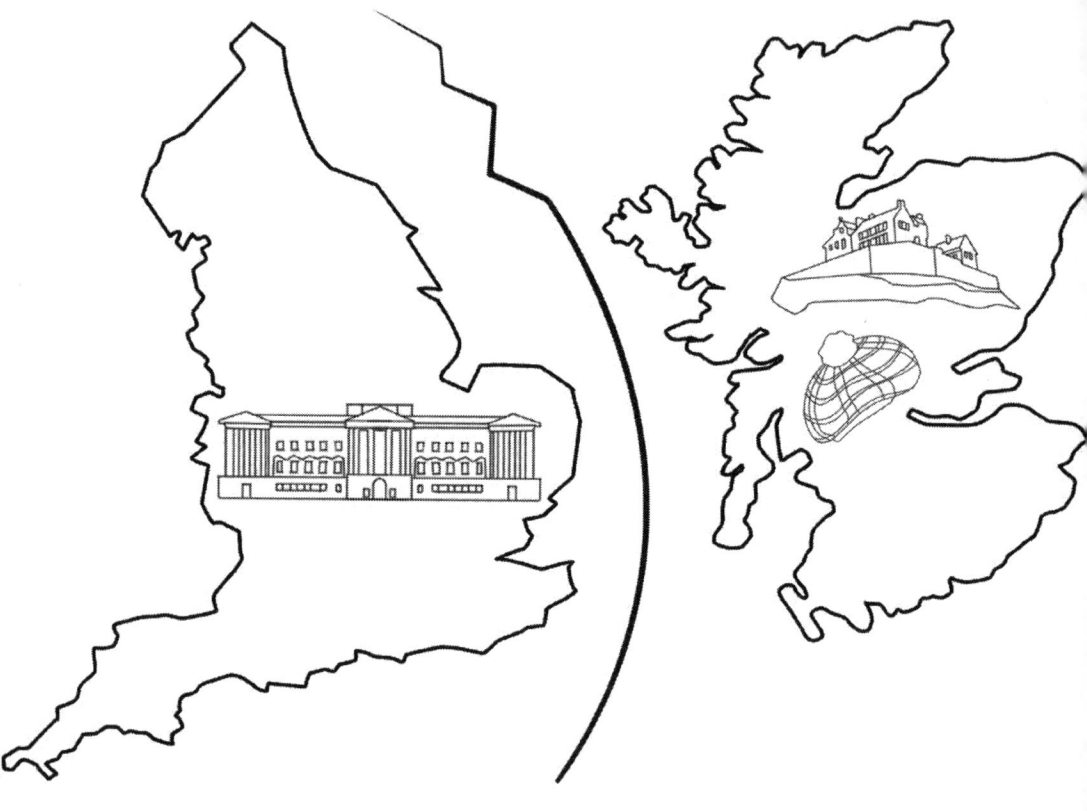

NO LONGER YOURS

We signed your pact in troubled days,
But now we see through painted praise.

A union forged in crown and chain -
You gave us roads; we bore the strain.

You took our oil, you claimed our seas,
And wrapped our hopes in policies.

You called it unity, called it fair -
But power sat in London's chair.

You scoffed at talk of going lone,
As if we'd crumble on our own.

But look around – what have we gained?
A voice ignored, a spirit drained.

We marched in wars we did not start,
Paid debts that broke our beating heart.

And we begged for just a say,
You laughed and turned the vote away.

No more, we say. We know our worth -
A land of fire, of song, of earth.

We are no fringe, nor child, nor toy -
We are a people, not your ploy.

The Saltire rises not in hate,
But in the hands that choose their fate.

We'll write our laws; we'll chart our course -
A nation free, by will, not force.

So, keep your pomp, your gilded show -
We've got our own path left to go.

And when we march, we march for truth -
For justice, voice and Scotland's youth.

SCOTLAND'S SHAME
A Failing Justice System

In courtrooms carved from stone and pride,
Where robes still march and laws abide,
They claim the scale is firm and fair-
But justice stumbles, unaware.

The Saltire flies, the thistle stands,
Yet blood still stains the court's own hands.
For crimes that tear our towns apart,
The sentences are soft at heart.

A life destroyed, a child in pain,
Yet killers stroll out dry from the rain.
With time served short and lessons thin,
The cycle turns; it starts again.

The judges speak with learned grace,
But rarely look at the victim's face.
Their words are cold, detached, refined-
While grief and rage burn in our mind.

A drunken fist, a broken bone-
"A year" they say, "Now off you go".
No jail, no weight, no fear instilled-
No sense that justice has been filled.

They preach reform, a second chance,
But fail to see their victim's stance.
Where's their reprieve, their fresh new page?
They're left with scars and silenced rage.

Oh Scotland, land of law so old,
With roots in history, proud and bold-
But if the law forgets it role,
Then mercy's price is far too toll.

We need a voice that stands and shouts,
That calls the coward system out.
Not vengeance, no – but rightful dues,
For those who maim, abuse, misuse.

Let justice rise with firmer hand,
Let law protect this weary land.
For till we match the crime with weight,
We're just repackaging the hate.

KAYDEN

For a boy who went to the beach and never came home

He ran where the wind met the sea,
Barefoot dreams where the gulls flew free-
Sixteen summers held in his hands,
Cut short on Ayrshire's golden sands.

A footballer's heart, fierce and bright,
He lit the pitch with laughter and fight.
Busby's pride, a brother's guide,
A grandson's echo, a father's stride.

But one moment broke the tide.
One blade, one act, one shattered sky.
What words can make the silence speak
Of blood spilled young on Irvine beach?

A town now grieves in hushed lament,
A school wears sorrow like cement.
His desk, his voice, his empty place,
The ghost of kindness in every face.

And his father writes through trembling hand:
My main man, you'll always stand.
In every breath, in every dream,
In places you were yet to be.

Scotland weeps with East Kilbride.
A wound too deep. A soul denied.
We say his name. We rage, we cry:
Kayden Moy-too young to die.

IN JUST TWO MONTHS

For Amen Teklay, Kayden Moy and every child lost too soon

In just two months, two lives were lost,
To blades that cut through more than frost.
Amen, just fifteen, fell in March-
On Glasgow's Street beneath the arch.

No warning bell, no time to run,
His story ended, barely begun.
Three boys arrested, young as him-
Innocence drowned, futures grim.

Ten weeks on, the pain still raw,
Kayden found on Irvine's shore.
Sixteen years, a beach, a knife-
Another boy stripped of his life.

Between these deaths, the toll runs high-
Eleven more hurt under Scotland's sky.
Sixteen teens cuffed, charged, or tried,
While parents ask, why has hope died?

A 13-year-old at Asda's door,
A blade in hand, still wanting more.
Two twelve-year-olds in Lenzie fight,
Left another boy bleeding in the night.

Stonehaven shook on March fifteen-
An 18-year-old stabbed on the green.
Eight days after, a child of eleven
Caught with a blade at a funfair heaven.

Kinghorn Beach-thirty in a mob,
Four boys battered, blood-soaked, robbed,
Portobello echoed with sirens' sound-
Three teens stabbed, dropped to the ground.

In Aberdeen, a girl of twelve
Cut by another-what dark spell
Turns children into sharpened rage,
And steel the ink on every page?

A seven-year-old, knife in class-
What lessons did we let him pass?
Three schools, three knifes, in children's hands-
Where did we lose the line we planned?

Two names carved into fresh-dug graves,
While headlines scroll like crashing waves.
Amen, Kayden. Just the start-
A nation tearing at its heart.

This isn't distant, isn't past-
These weeks have sliced through us so fast.
How many more must we allow?
To fall beneath what we allow?

What justice sleeps while young blood spills?
What silence keeps us standing still?
If two months wrought this bloody toll,
We've lost control. We've lost control.

Love Poems

A MOTHER'S LOVE

In quiet shadows, self-doubt creeps,
Where whispered thoughts like secrets seep.
Did choice and love weave paths so wide,
Or pull me closer, filled with pride?

Four lanterns born of love's own spark,
Guiding my way through the deep and the dark.
With every laugh, each tear you share,
You teach me strength beyond compare.
I wear my heart upon my sleeve,

A tapestry of dreams of dreams we weave.
Each tender moment, each shared embrace,
A treasure held in time and space.
Am I enough in this wild dance,

In sleepless nights and fleeting chances?
Yet in your smiles, I find my grace,
A fierce devotion, a sacred place.
With every step, I pledge to shield,

Through storms of doubt, my love, revealed.
I stand, unwavering, brave and tall,
For you, my dears, I'd risk it all.
So, when the night grows dark and deep,
Know in my heart, my love you'll keep.

For in your laughter, I find my way,
Four beautiful souls, my light each day.
And when the years draw near their close,
With all my strength, your dreams I'll chase.
In your bright futures, I'll see the spark,
A mother's love forever marked.

CHILDHOOD PAIN

In shadows cast by childhood pain,
A woman stands with heart in chain,
Abuse that once left her so broken,
Now echoes through her roles unspoken.

As mother, she strives to be complete,
Yet fears she is failing at every feat,
The ghost of past mistakes resounds,
A constant whisper, "you're not enough around"

She recalls the words that cut so deep,
"You'll never be the one they keep",
Those scars now reopened wide,
Each time she looks into her children's eyes.

Her marriage too, the fear is there,
The weight of expectation high and steep,
A wife who feels like she's asleep.

But still, she rises each new day,
To face the challenges along the way,
Though doubts creep in with every fall,
She finds strength in the love for them all.

With every step, a voice grows clear,
A whisper telling her to persevere,
That though her path was once defined by strife,
She is more than the life she lived in her youth.

And as she looks upon her family dear,
She realizes she's held back tears,
For in their smiles, her strength is found,
A love that heals, a heart unbound.

Through trials, she discovers might,
A resilience born for endless night,
A phoenix rising, wings outstretched wide,
No longer bound, she begins to glide.

SCOTLAND MY HOME

Scotland, a place I call my own,
With rolling hills where wild winds have blown,
Misty mornings in a gentle embrace,
In every corner, I find a trace.

Blue blood runs through these ancient lands,
Proudly we stand with our clan's strong hands,
In tartan wraps and with bagpipes tune,
Under the watch of a silver moon.

The thistle blooms where the brave hearts tread,
With stories of heroes long since fled,
Breathtaking scenery, a painter's dream,
In every valley, a soft, silent scream.

No Scotland, no party, the saying rings clear,
For joy is a treasure when friends gather near,
With laughter and warmth, our spirits entwine,
In the heart of this land, where stars brightly shine.

The echoes of laughter on cobblestone streets,
In pubs filled with love, where friendships complete,
Each stranger a Neighbour, each smile a grace,
In the heart of this kingdom, I've found my place.

From Highland to Lowland, the beauty astounds,
In forests and glens where the spirit surrounds,
The history whispers in the winds that do wail,
In every stone's story, a rustic tale.

Oh Scotland, my heart beats in rhythm with thee,
In every sunrise, I feel wild and free,
A land of deep roots, where my soul finds its way,
In this tapestry woven, I'll forever stay.

So, raise up your glass to the hills and the skies,
To friendships that flourish and never say goodbyes,
For in this embrace, I am never alone,
In Scotland, the place I proudly call home.

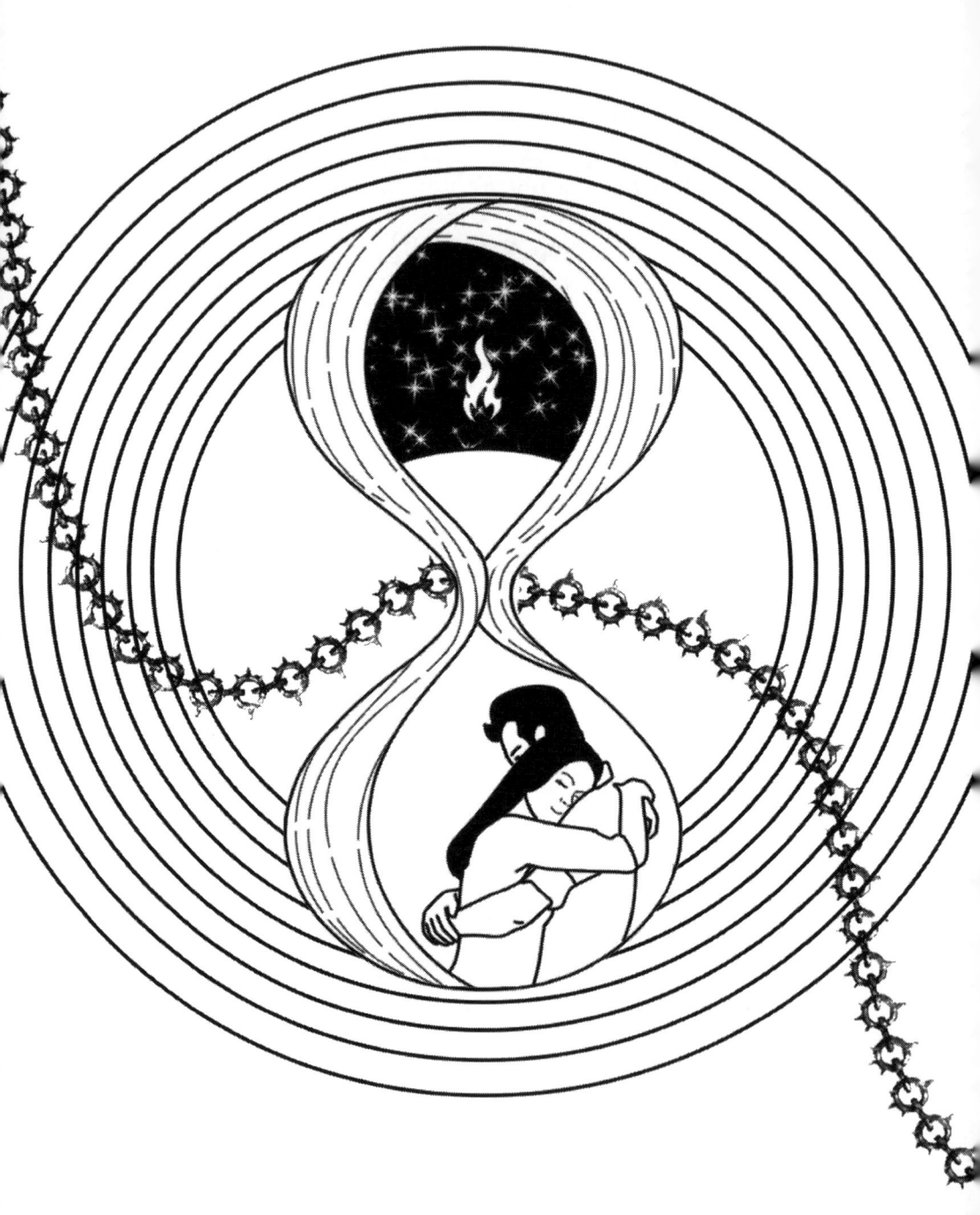

ETERNAL US

We are not bound by clocks,
Nor measured in years.
Time folds around us -
Creases of a paper that never tears.

Your soul has known mine
Long before this skin,
Like rivers recognizing
The pull of the sea.

Every glance,
A translation of a language
Only we can speak.
Every touch,
A reminder -
We have been here before.

Even when silence falls heavy,
It is soft between us.
Even when distance stretches,
I find you in the quiet.

We are not temporary.
We are the echo and the origin,
The spark and the ember,
The promise that survives
Every ending.

If the stars should burn out,
If the earth should fold in on itself,
Still-
Your soul and mine
Will stand hand in hand,
A love that does not end,
Only continues.

STILL, YOU RISE

Life isn't always gentle,
Sometimes it stings before it sings -
Throws storms across your sky,
And dares you to keep walking through the rain.

But look at you,
Still standing,
Still breathing,
Still showing up.

That's power,
Not in perfection, but in persistence
Not in having all the answers,
But in asking the questions anyway.

You've known endings that broke your heart,
But here you are -
Writing new beginnings
With hands that once trembled but never let go.

The truth is:
You are the sky, not the storm.
You are the roots, not the wind.
You are the fire that keeps burning
Even when no one sees the flame.

So live.
Not just in survival, but in joy, in wonder,
In the quiet strength of choosing yourself every single day.

Because life is not about being unbreakable.
It's about being beautifully bent, and still – rising!

THIS LOVE, THIS LIFE

I used to think love had to be loud -
Fireworks, grand gestures,
Hearts racing like trains in the night.
But then you walked in,
Soft as sunrise
And suddenly
Peace felt like passion, too.

This love?
It's not a storm -
It's a shelter.
Not a burning match,
But a steady flame
That warms a cold day
And never asks for more than truth.

You touch my chaos
Like it's sacred.
You see the cracks,
And still,
You trace them like constellations -
Proof that I've survived,
That I'm art and not just aftermath.

Life with you
Isn't perfect,
But it's real.
It's shared silence over morning coffee,
Dancing in the kitchen to no music,
Messy hair, deep talks,
And knowing looks across the room
That say, I see you, I'm still here.

I used to chase happiness,
Like it was something far away.
But now,
I find it
Right here,
In your hands,
In this moment,
In this love,
This quiet,
Unshakeable,
Beautiful life.

WHERE MY HEART WRITES

I write because I have to feel,
To make the fleeting moments real.
A melody, a verse, a rhyme -
I shape my soul in lines of time.

Words come softly, like a breeze,
Or crash like storms upon the seas.
They live in every breath I miss.

A song begins with just one thought,
A truth that lingers, gently caught.
A poem spills from midnight dreams,
From quiet sighs and silent screams.

This is my voice, my way to cope,
To build a bridge, to craft some hope.
To hold the light, to touch the ache,
To say the things, I cannot fake.

With every line, I'm set more free -
The truest, rawest form of me.
I write to live, I write to be,
And through my words, the world can see.

So let the pages fill and grow,
With all the depths I've come to know.
My love is loud, yet softly sown -
In every song or poem, I've found my home.

THROUGH MY LENS

I see the world in frames of light,
In golden dawns and soft twilight.
A shutter clicks, a moment caught -
A whisper held, a fleeting thought.

The smallest things, they speak to me -
A shadow stretched, a dancing tree.
A wrinkled hand, a laughing glance,
The stillness in a child's stance.

My camera is my quiet voice,
It captures truth, it gives me choice.
To freeze the chaos, find the grace -
To hold the soul of time and place.

Each photo tells a tale I knew,
But also paints a world brand new.
A love, a storm, a breath, a spark -
A candle glowing in the dark.

For when I shoot, I truly see,
Not just the world – but more of me -
In every frame, my heart takes flight -
To turn the ordinary into light.

So let me roam, just let me find
The beauty others leave behind.
Through lens and light, I chase and show
The love I carry, shot in glow.

WHERE LOVE BEGINS

It starts in silence, soft and slow,
A glance that warms the world you know.
A breath you didn't know you held,
Released where something sweet has dwelled.

No fireworks, no grand parade-
Just sunlight shifting through the shade.
A smile that lingers, eyes that shine,
And hands that somehow slip in mine.

The hours stretch and then collapse,
In quiet talks and laughter's lapse.
The air between us hums and sings,
Alive with slow, unfolding things.

Your voice becomes my favourite sound,
My thoughts drift where your name is found.
Each touch, a promise yet unspoken,
Each look, a vow that won't be broken.

It's not a fall but more a flight,
A tethered soul set free to light.
And all the world, once cold and wide,
Now gently turns with you inside.

This is the grace that lovers find:
Two hearts no longer misaligned.
A tender truth, a sacred art-
The falling in of heart to heart.

THE JOY BETWEEN THE PAGES
FOR MY GRANDAD WHO GAVE ME
THE GIFT OF STORIES

A book is like a secret door,
That opens wide to so much more.
From quiet nooks to distant lands,
I travel far without a plan.

Danielle Steel, with heart and grace,
Takes me to a softer place -
Where love is fierce and dreams are strong,
And even sorrow finds its song.

My grandad smiled and said, "Just Read"
And planted in my soul that seed.
Now every chapter, every line,
Feels like a gift that once was mine.

When stories end, I feel the sting-
As though I've lost a precious thing.
But that's the magic books can lend;
They let you live, then miss a friend.

Each cover holds a world brand new,
With skies of gold and oceans blue.
The pages turn, the real world fades,
And joy comes dancing through the shades.

So, I will read, and laugh, and cry,
And lift my head to meet the sky.
For books are more than words and ink,
They give us wings and time to think.

Loss Poems

DUNBLANE

March thirteenth, a day of dread,
Dunblane's peace, so cruelly shed.
A gym, a place of joyful sound,
Turned silent, horror all around.

Thomas Hamilton, a shadowed name,
Brought darkness, fuelled by wicked flame.
Sixteen young lives, so pure, so bright,
Extinguished in the morning's light.

A teacher brave, a shield of grace,
Protecting children, in that place,
Their innocence, a cruel demise,
Reflected in their tear-filled eyes.

Fifteen more, the wounds they bear,
A memory etched beyond compare.
Primary one, so small, so sweet,
Their tiny lives, a bitter defeat.

Scotland's heart, a broken thing,
Forever mourning, sorrow's sting.
They're angels now, beyond the pain,
Too beautiful for earthly rain.

The guns he held, a dreadful tool,
Shattered lives yet broke no rule.
A morning born of darkest night,
Dunblane's sorrow, burning bright.

I DON'T KNOW WHY I DO THIS

I wake up angry.
It's like the sun burns me
Before it even rises,
Everything feels too loud,
Too sharp,
Too much.

You stand in the doorway -
Same tired eyes,
Same soft voice trying to be firm,
And I hate you for it.
I hate you for trying
When all I want is to fall apart.

You ask me what's wrong
I don't know,
I never know,
But it feels like a storm inside me,
And you're the nearest thing to break.

So, I say the cruellest thing I can think of,
"I wish you were dead"
I see how it hits you -
The flinch in your face,
The silence that follows.
But I don't take it back,
I can't.

I shove my sisters away.
They don't get it.
They still believe in birthdays and hugs.
They still believe in me.
I don't.

I run.
From you, from home.
From the voice inside that tells me
I'm not enough,
Never was,
Never will be.
I threaten the end
Because sometime
It feels like the only thing I can control.

You call it manipulation
I call it drowning

I push every wall just to feel something solid.
But I hate myself after.
I see your tears,
The way you beg me to come back,
And I wonder why you even bother.

But part of me...
Part of me wants you to hold on.
Part of me wants to crawl in your lap like I used to
When monsters were only in books
And I believed you could fix anything.

I'm sorry.
Even if I don't say it
I am.

I don't know how to stop this.
But please -
Don't stop loving me.
Not yet

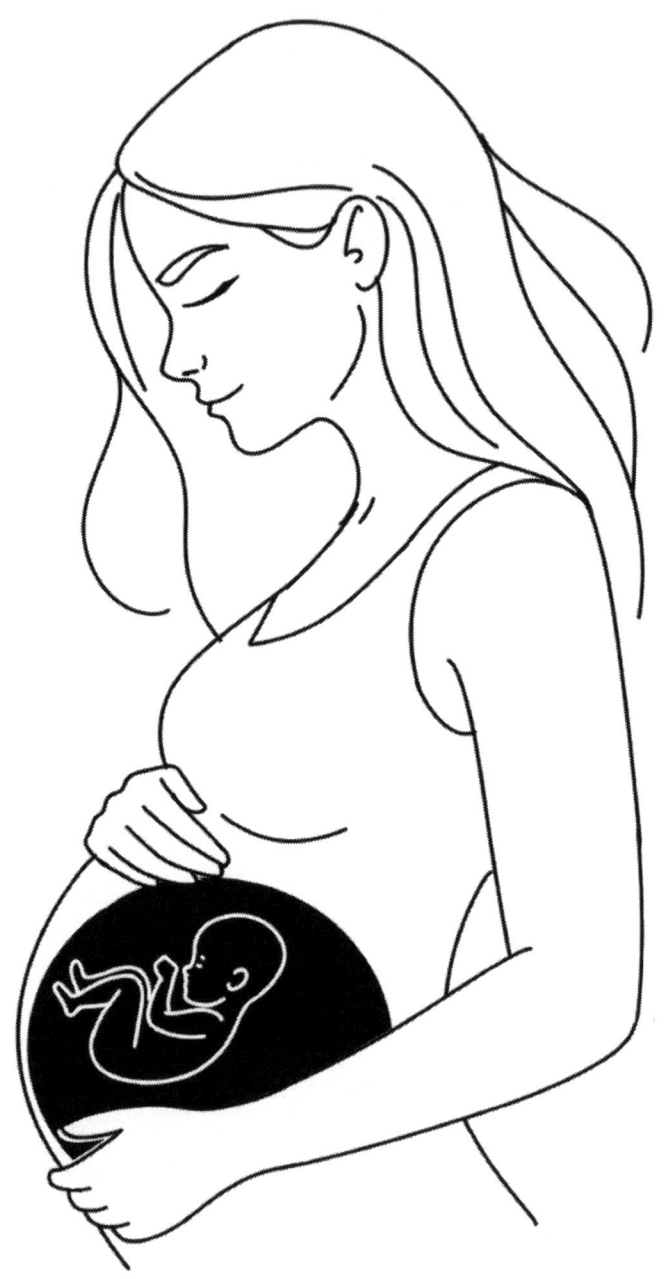

THIRTEEN WEEKS

I never held you close or tight,
Or rocked you softly through the night.
No lullabies, no tiny cries-
Just shattered dreams and silent skies.

Thirteen weeks along, and yet I knew,
You were my son, my heart, my view.
They said, "It's early", like that made
The ache less sharp, the loss less weighed.

But love begins before the birth,
In quiet hope and growing worth.
I pictured you with eyes like mine,
A life ahead, a steady line.

And then-just gone, no warning sign.
No reason, sense, or sacred sign.
They called it chance, they called it fate,
But none of that could change the weight.

I raged, I wept, I fell apart,
I mourned you with a mother's heart.
Though tiny, still you changed my soul,
You made a space I can't make whole.

Thirteen long years, and still you stay,
In thoughts that never drift away.
In quiet hours, when no one sees,
You rise again on every breeze.

No birthdays came, no toys, no shoes,
Just love and grief I didn't choose.
But still I say, with voice held high:
You lived, you mattered, and you lie

Beneath my ribs, within my chest-
A name the world can't quite digest.
But I will say it, bold and true-
My son, my love, I carry you.

THE PARK BENCH LIED

She thought she'd found a friend that day,
A smile that seemed to light the grey-
Fourteen years, a voice so sweet,
Inviting her to where they'd meet.

The younger girl, just twelve and shy,
With starlight hope behind each eye.
She trusted words, believed the face,
And followed to that open place.

But kindness cracked like brittle stone,
The older girl was not alone-
Her fists were fury, boots were hate,
And violence sealed the younger's fate.

A playground turned to battleground,
No laughter there, no friendly sound.
A golf ball lump upon her head,
Two swollen eyes, near left for dead.

They called the aid, they rushed her fast,
But scars like these are built to last.
Concussed and broken, dazed and torn,
A childhood lost, a soul forlorn.

Now fifteen, she won't go outside,
Still haunted by the day she cried.
The park, the world-it's not the same,
She flinches at her very name.

The girl who hurt her? Still walks free.
Now sixteen, no apology.
Though seven more have felt her wrath,
The law just cleared her bloody path.

No cell, no charge, no lessons learned,
While justice sleeps and silence burns.
What price for pain? What weight for fear?
The system shrugs; it's nowhere near.

But in the shadows, voices rise-
We write the truth they still disguise.
For every child who's been betrayed,
This poem stands, unafraid.

BREAKING THE CHAIN

It doesn't roar-it whispers low,
A quiet pull you hardly know.
A touch, a taste, a fleeting high,
Then all you do is chase the sky.

It wraps around your every breath,
A slow, familiar kind of death.
You lie, you fall, you lose your name,
And swear each time won't end the same.

You know the dark, you know the cost,
The time, the trust, the things you've lost.
But somewhere beneath the ache,
A voice still fights; a heart won't break.

You claw your way through bitter night,
Afraid, alone, but craving light.
You fall. You rise. You fall again-
But still, you curse the weight, the chain.

Each small step is a rebel cry,
A truth you hold when cravings lie.
Recovery's not clean or kind-
It's war within your own worn mind.

But strength is born in fractured places,
In weary hands and tear-streaked faces.
So, keep the fight, however slow-
You're more than what you used to know.

You're not the bottle, not the blade,
Not every bad choice that you made.
You are the storm that doesn't drown-
The soul that falls, then turns around.

GRANNY AGNES
25 YEARS IN OUR HEARTS
– 2ND JUNE 2000

A tiny wee woman, so gentle, so bright,
Yet you filled up our world with your warmth and your light.
You stood just so small, but your love stood so tall,
You were everything, everything – heart, soul, and all.

Four children you helped to grow, guide, and adore,
You and our Di – we needed no more.
With biscuits in your hands and a hug at the door,
You gave us a love that will live evermore.

The Telly would baffle, the HI-FI would squeal,
But Daniel O'Donnell still made your day real.
Murray Mints tucked in your pockets so deep,
And stories you whispered to help us all to sleep.

Then came the heartbreak, too heavy to bear -
We lost our dear Di, and then you weren't there.
Two guiding lights gone in six cruel months' time,
It felt like the world had forgotten its rhyme.

At thirteen, I broke – we all broke that day,
The grief didn't soften; it just found its way.
It was more than a goodbye, more than a part,
We lost the two souls who had built up our hearts.

And now twenty-five years have quietly passed,
But the ache in our chest will forever last.
We still see you, Gran, in small, sacred ways -
In sweet, silent moments and soft childhood days.

You were home, you were hugs, you were sugar and song,
You were where we belonged all our whole lives along.
And though we keep walking, though time marches through,
We carry a piece of our hearts lost with you.

Granny Agnes, our anchor, our peace,
Your love was a shelter; your spirit won't cease.
A quarter of a century, yet still we say true-
We miss you; we love you; we still look for you.

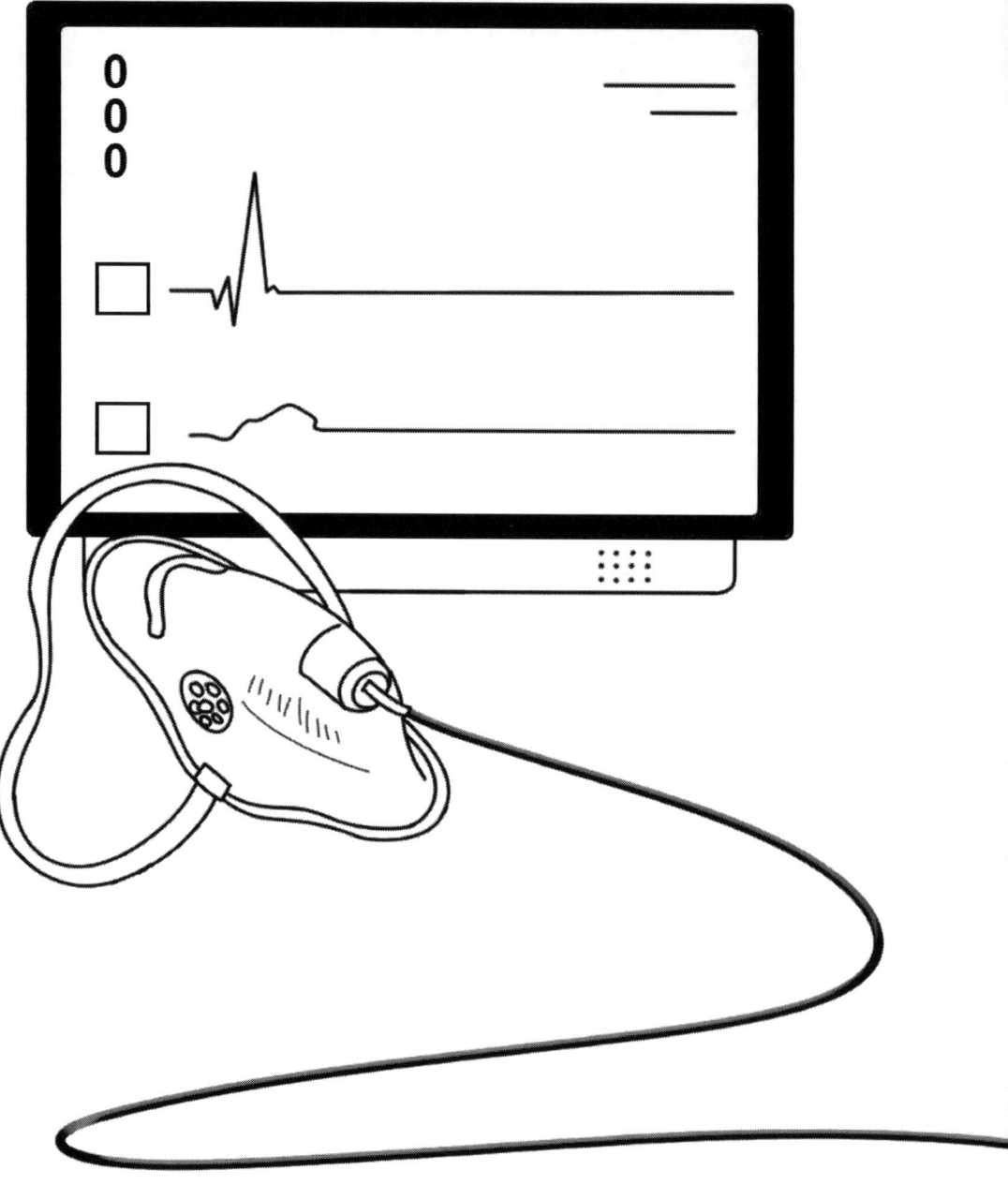

WAITING FOR THE CALL

She walked in alone just a week ago,
Still standing, still fighting, not ready to go.
Now they say "days" like time's running thin -
And I wait for the moment the end rushes in.

She's not my mother, but she's part of my soul,
She made us a family; she made broken things whole.
My husband's first love, my girl's safe embrace,
Now cancer is stealing her light from this place.

The phone doesn't ring – but it will. I can tell.
That silence before it feels heavy as hell.
Each second is glass that I walk on and bleed,
Still hoping for mercy, still drowning in need.

My husband just breaks without making a sound,
Grief pulling his world down to the ground.
His eyes are so tired, his hands always shake -
He's losing the one no one can ever fake.

Our eldest eighteen, still thinks this can mend -
Still believes "Granny gets better" in the end.
She smiles, she hums, but she doesn't quite see
That some goodbyes come too quietly.

Sixteen stays strong, but I know it's a mask,
She folds all her sorrow into small tasks.
Fourteen just stares at the space on the wall,
Like she's bracing herself for the sound of the call.

And twelve, just mutters, "It's shit".
Then wipes her red eyes and pretends she's fine with it.
They're too young for this, too soft to be torn -
But death doesn't care how young you were born.

And me – I'm just trying to carry them through,
While waiting for news that will cut me in two.
I'm wife and I'm mother, and now, in this role,
I carry their heartbreak and still pay the toll.

She's leaving us slowly, her breath growing light,
Her body is here, but her soul's taking flight.
And I want it to end, and I don't all at once.
How do you let go of someone who loves?

She's not my mum, but oh, she was near -
Closer than blood, more fierce than fear.
She raised the man who now breaks in my arms,
She gave me my girls, gave our home all its charm.

So, I sit in the quiet, my heart in a vice,
Trading each moment for grief's asking price.
The phone will ring soon, and I'll answer that sound -
And know that her body is cold in the ground.

But tonight, she's still breathing, still barely alive -
And I whisper, "Please stay, please try to survive".
Just one more sunrise, one more kiss goodnight -
Before we fall into endless night.

OUR GRIEF

The girls are lost in grief's dark tide,
Teenage hearts with no place to hide.
My husband's eyes, in disbelief,
Cannot accept this weight of grief.

Eileen is gone – how can that be true?
Her window's smile, her daily view,
The TV hum, her gentle wave,
All memories we cannot save.

No head popped in to say, "I'm here",
No quiet presence, warm and near.
The little things now hurt the most,
Each tender moment haunts like ghosts.

We plan her songs, her flowers bright,
Her favourite pink, her final night.
The tea, the food, the mournful tone,
To honour her yet feel alone.

This drowning sorrow pulls me down,
A broken heart that cannot drown.
It breaks for her, for the girls, for him,
Yet Eileen's love will not grow dim.

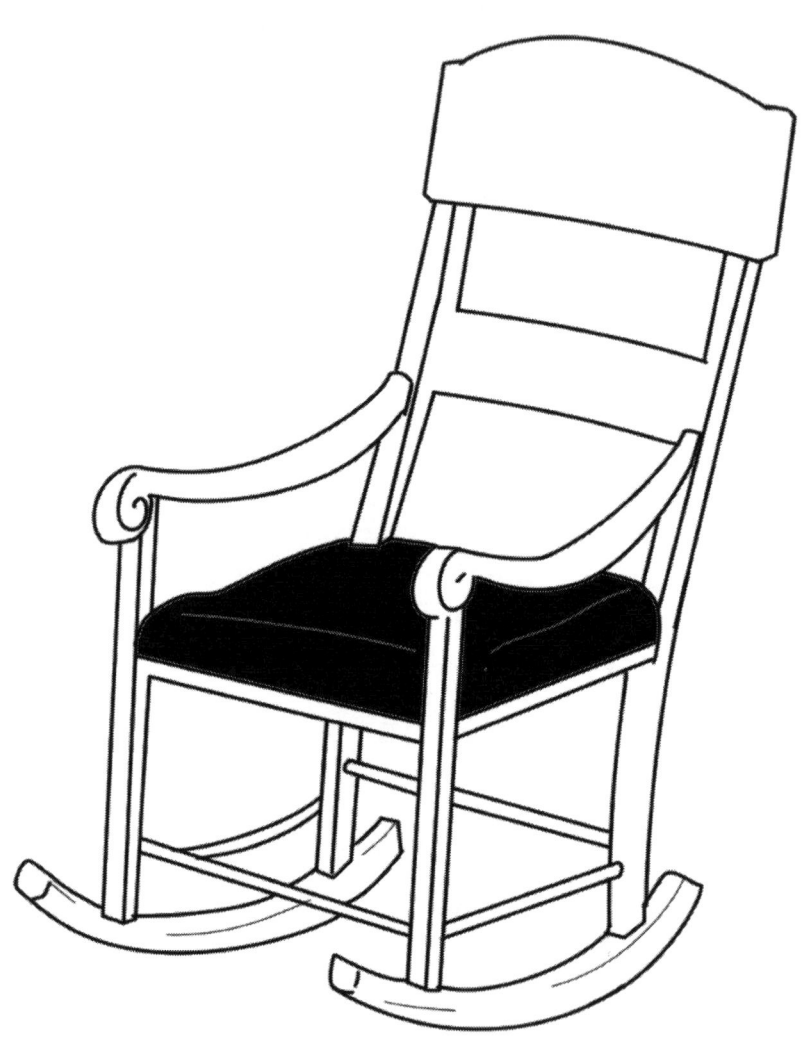

FOR EILEEN

We gather here in shadows deep,
To grieve, to love, to softly weep.
Our hearts are heavy, torn in two,
Eileen, this day we honour you.

The girls are wrapped in sorrow's tide,
Teenage hearts with no place to hide.
My husband stands in disbelief,
Her son, who bears the sharpest grief.

No more gentle smiles through the window,
No wave, no laugh, no pause awhile.
No quiet knock upon the door,
No simple joys we shared before.

Her favourite shows, her favourite chair,
The little ways she showed her care.
It's these small things we'll miss the most,
Each now a cherished, tender ghost.

We plan her songs, her colours bright,
Her pinks, her blooms, her guiding light.
The tea, the food, the voices near,
All gathered just because she's dear.

It feels like drowning, sorrow's sea,
A weight of love and memory.
Yet through the pain, her light still stays,
Eileen walks with us always.

For though her voice we cannot hear,
Her presence lingers, warm and clear.
In every laugh, in every smile,
She'll walk beside us all the while.

So let us grieve, but let us see,
The gift she left – her legacy.
Through love she gave, so pure, so true,
You'll carry Eileen's heart with you.

THE DAY AFTER

Mum,
Yesterday, the sun shone over Fife,
As if it didn't know
We were breaking apart.
The graveyard was still,
Just us, the stone, the sky -
And two songs to carry you.

"Memories" played,
And every word cut sharp,
As though it was written
For this very moment,
For us standing there,
Unable to let go.
And then "Bye Bye Baby"
To close -
A song too sweet for such a day,
But it lifted you,
And it broke us all at once.

Today, the light has gone.
The sky is grey,
The cold bites deep into the garden.
I pass your annex by the back door -
So near, so empty.
Your chair waits,
The blanket folded,
The space humming with your absence.
I almost knock,
As if you might still call out,
As if music and memory
Could bring you back.

How can yesterday hold the sun
And today be nothing but cloud?
How can the ground take you
When the songs still ring in my chest?
The girls are quiet,
Gary is lost in thought,
And I stand by the door
Listening for a voice
That will never come again.

The day after a funeral
Is colder than the graveyard.
It is silence where your laughter should be,
A back door that will never open,
And two songs that will
Forever carry your name.

Life Poems

TEENAGE JUNGLE, POPULATION: ME

Adulthood, for me,
Is surviving four hormonal hurricanes
Under one roof.

I used to dream of classrooms -
Now I negotiate peace treaties
Over who stole whose mascara
(or whose hoodie that definitely isn't communal)

The Wi-Fi goes down for five minutes
And it's apocalypse-level panic:
"MUUUUUM! Do something!"
As if I secretly control the internet
From a switch in my pocket.

The fridge?
A crime scene.
Milk vanished, bread massacred,
Yoghurt pots abandoned like clues.
And somehow-
Despite four suspects-
No one ate the last biscuit.

My ears are filled with the holy trinity:
"I'm bored."
"You don't get it."
And the classic,
"Can you take me to [insert social event thirty seconds before leaving]?"

Laundry multiplies like rabbits.
There's glitter on the sofa,
Eyeliner on the bathroom tiles,
And an unidentified smell
Coming from one bedroom
I dare not name.

But then-
Mid-chaos-
They'll crack a joke so sharp
I choke on my coffee,
Or flop beside me on the bed
Pretending it's "just because"
(They still like a cuddle
They just won't admit it).

So yes,
I live in a madhouse.
I'm ringmaster, referee,
And reluctant Uber driver.
But if chaos is the currency of love,
I'm filthy rich.

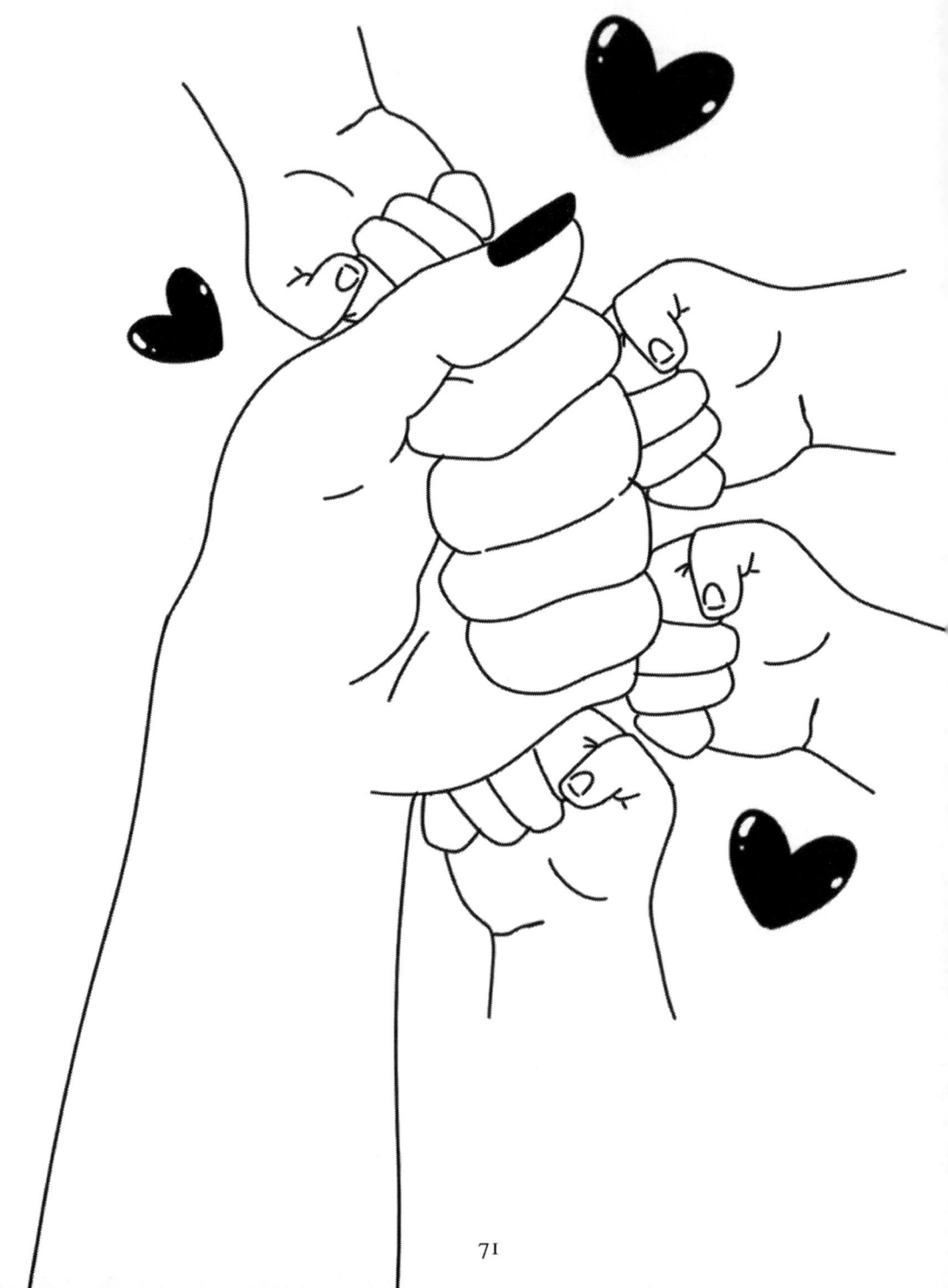

NO OTHER WAY

I remember me, small and wild,
a tangle of dreams, scraped knees,
and quiet moments no one noticed.
A million paths stretched out like rivers,
each one calling,
each one promising something different.

I see the choices—
the mistakes, the heartbreaks, the stumbles,
the nights I cried alone
and the mornings I laughed like nothing mattered.
I see the joys—
the unexpected moments,
the triumphs that tasted like sunlight,
the love that found me anyway.

And I would not change a single thing.
Every turn, every wrong step,
every perfect accident
led me to this exact point,
to a life I never dared imagine:

Four daughters, loud and alive,
each one a heartbeat in a different rhythm,
two dogs who bark at the world,
a husband who makes home feel like a hug,
and me, finally understanding
that all the paths I didn't take
were just guides,
leading me straight to here.

I would not change a single tear,
nor a single laugh,
because every one of them
built this messy, beautiful, unshakable now.

And I would stay here forever,
because I am exactly where I belong—
and I would be nowhere else.

FOR HOLLY, WITH THE MISCHIEF SMILE

At three years old, so small, so bright,
She faced the dark yet shone with light.
While needles came and medicines flowed,
She danced along a heavy road.

A tiny frame, a warrior's soul,
With laughter stitched into the whole.
Though pain would knock and fear drew near,
She met it all with joy, not fear.

We watched, our hearts in silent ache,
Afraid of how much one could take.
She came so close to slipping free-
The moment nearly shattered me.

But Holly smiled-oh, how she shone,
With spark and mischief her own.
She showed us strength we'd never known,
In every breath, in every bone.

The years rolled on, she found her peace,
But storms like hers don't always cease.
At ten, it rose again to fight,
Yet she stood tall, a beam of light.

Another year, another test,
And still she smiled, still gave her best.
With quiet grace and steady flame,
She wore her courage like her name.

She is the sun through darkest skies,
The reason tears still cleanse our eyes.
She is the storm that learns to sing,
The gentle might of everything.

Oh Holly, child of fire and grace,
With mischief dancing on your face-
You've taught us how to rise and stand,
To hold the world with open hand.

You are the miracle we see,
The heart of all we'll ever be.
And though the road was steep and wild-
You met it all, our fearless child.

TATTOO

Ink flows like a river, deep and wide,
Each stroke a story, each mark a pride.
A canvas on skin, my tale to tell,
In pain, beauty blossoms; I wear it well.

Skulls whisper secrets of life and death,
In their shadowed gaze, I find my breath.
Emblems of strength, of battles I've faced,
In every design, my essence embraced.

Why do I do it, this dance with the blade?
To capture my soul in the art that I crave.
Each needle's embrace, a moment defined,
A reflection of spirit, a glimpse of my mind.

Tattooed tributes to who I have been,
In colours and shapes, my journey begins.
With every new ink, I evolve and grow,
A beautiful tapestry, a story to show.

So let them ask why, let them all stare,
For these markings I wear, speak of love and care.
In pain there is beauty, in skulls there is grace,
This is my personality, my heart in this space.

THE PROM QUEEN IN BLUE

She stood in blue, a quiet flame,
A whispered heart, a cherished name.
Eighteen years of gentle grace,
With stars reflected in her face.

Shy of crowds, but not of dreams,
She stepped into the evening's gleam.
A sky of silk, the softest hue,
Her eyes, twin oceans deep and true.

The world can feel too loud, too fast -
But Hannah stood, she faced it, passed.
Five foot ten of strength unseen,
A warrior dressed like a queen.

Her father's eyes told all that night -
A look of love, of fierce delight.
No words were said, yet still we knew
How proud he was of all she grew.

From tiny hands to trembling heels,
She danced where once she feared to feel.
A moment wrapped in laughter's light,
A daughter blooming into flight.

And as the music filled the air,
She wasn't just there – SHE WAS THERE!
Not hidden in a shadowed place,
But radiant, in her own space.

So, here's to Hannah – brave and bright -
A soul who found her wings that night.
And to the dad whose eyes confessed
The quiet truth: she is my best.

SCREEN-BOUND

We used to run, we used to play,
Climb the trees and race all day.
But now we sit with faces bright,
Lit by screens that steal the night.

Heads are down, the world goes past,
Moments fading far too fast.
We scroll and we tap; we click and stare-
But miss the life that's really there.

Friends are dots on glowing glass,
Voices lost as moments pass.
We laugh in text, not in the room,
Our silence growing like a tomb.

A thousand pics, a thousand views,
Yet still we wear comparison's shoes.
Chasing likes like they're our worth,
Forgetting joy is found on earth.

We've lost the art of looking up,
Of sharing stories, tea in cup.
Of feeling wind, of touching the rain,
Of healing hearts through real pain.

So, take a stand, unplug a while,
Look around, breathe, walk a mile.
The world is here, it's loud, it's real-
More than a post, more than a reel.

Lift your eyes and you will see,
Life begins beyond the screen.

LOOK AGAIN

You see her walk, six feet in frame,
With red curls wild, too big to tame.
Red glasses flash; her boots are black-
She doesn't flinch; she won't look back.

You think you know her, think she's loud,
Too much, too tall, too damn unbowed.
But what you miss behind the eyes
Is where her quiet thunder lies.

She smiles, but hides the war inside-
The anxious voice she can't outride.
The fear that if she dares reveal,
You'll mock the parts she'd hoped to heal.

She holds back tears with practiced grace,
Afraid to show her truest face.
But don't mistake her guarded tone-
She's built from fire and steel and bone.

She mothers four with love so wide,
No storm can break what's held inside.
She lifts their world with hands that shake-
And still finds more for others' sake.

You judge her shape, the way she moves?
Your silence cuts, but she improves.
She rises every time she's bruised-
She's not some woman you can use.

You do not see the fights she's won,
The night she stayed when others'd run.
The way she speaks, though fear is near-
She dares to live, despite the fear.

So if you look, then look again-
You're facing more than mortal skin.
She's rage and hope and ash and flame-
A woman proud to bear her name.

She doesn't need your soft applause,
She writes her worth in her own laws.
And every scar, and every fall-
Just makes her rise more fierce, more tall.

So let them judge, and let them sneer-
She walks through fire, year by year.
And still she stands, and still she'll say;
"I am this bold. I'll stay this way.

THE ONE WHO DIDN'T HOLD THE MIC

She never stood upon a stage,
No spotlight claimed her name,
But still she carved through the silence,
And set the world aflame.

With pen in hand, she drew our truth,
From places raw and real,
She gave our pain a platform,
She helped the nation feel.

When others turned their faces,
And systems shut their doors,
She opened up her pages
And made our voices roar.

My daughter's words rang through her work,
No longer lost or small,
And in her ink, a fire burned-
It echoed through us all.

As a parent, I was breaking,
With no place safe to stand,
But she heard me in the darkness,
And gently took my hand.

She carried every broken name,
Each headline drenched in grief,
But never let the weight of it
Diminish her belief.

She stood behind the story,
She never sought the fame,
Yet it was she who made them listen,
Who made them say our name.

The summit rose because she stayed,
When others walked away-
She fought for change with every breath,
And still, she does today.

So, here's to her – the quiet storm,
The strength we didn't see,
Who bled for every shattered youth,
And wrote us into history.

Not just a voice – but a vessel,
Of truth, of hope, of light -
She made sure we were heard.
She made sure we could fight.

THEN & NOW

I look out the window, the streets have changed,
The world I knew feels rearranged.
Back then, we played with sticks and stones,
Now screens glow bright in every home.

We ran through fields, so wide and free,
With skates and bikes, we chased the breeze.
Now voices buzz through apps and phones,
The laughter's quiet, we play alone.

CDs spun, mixtapes we made,
Cartoons at eight, we stayed up late,
Now every song streams with a click,
And instant fame comes fast, too quick.

No posters to pin, no walls to show,
Our heroes come to life, not just a glow.
Now every trend moves fast, moves high,
A child can blink and miss the sky.

Yet still I watch, through glass so clear,
The world keeps changing, year by year.
Though youth is different, strange somehow,
I smile at then and greet the now.

SHE WRITES

She was born where the walls would tremble and sway,
Where love came in shouting, then drifted away.
Where silence could cut like a whispering blade,
And kindness was rare as the warmth of May.

Her mother drank storms and let them cascade
On young, aching shoulders, alone and afraid.
She never asked thunder to fall from the skies,
But still bore the weight under tear-salted eyes.

She learned that trust is a word carved out in stone-
Left out in the rain, eroded, alone.
She gave hers to hands that vowed to stay,
But they shattered her trust and then walked away.

At thirteen, her world didn't fully fall down,
But something inside her refused to be found.
She stopped seeking mirrors, stopped seeking sound,
Felt sure that no soul would hear if she drowned.

Bur deep in the dark, she found ink and a page-
A space to release her quietest rage.
She wrote to survive, let sorrow flow,
To dream of a world where kind hands would grow.

Word upon word, she built from the pain,
A self, made of fire, of hope, of the rain.
She grew-not just older-but fiercely and right,
A warrior shaped in the absence of light.

Now she's a mother, a woman, a flame,
Who shields her own from sorrow and shame.
She listens, she holds, she stands strong and true,
Becoming the love she never once knew.

The past still whispers, but cannot command;
It doesn't define her, it doesn't stand.
She writes-not to flee, but to chart the climb,
Each line a reminder: she rose every time.

She tells the girl hidden deep in her mind,
"We made it, we lived, we rose, and we're kind.
The monsters are silent-they don't get the end.
We write the last word, with strength as our pen."

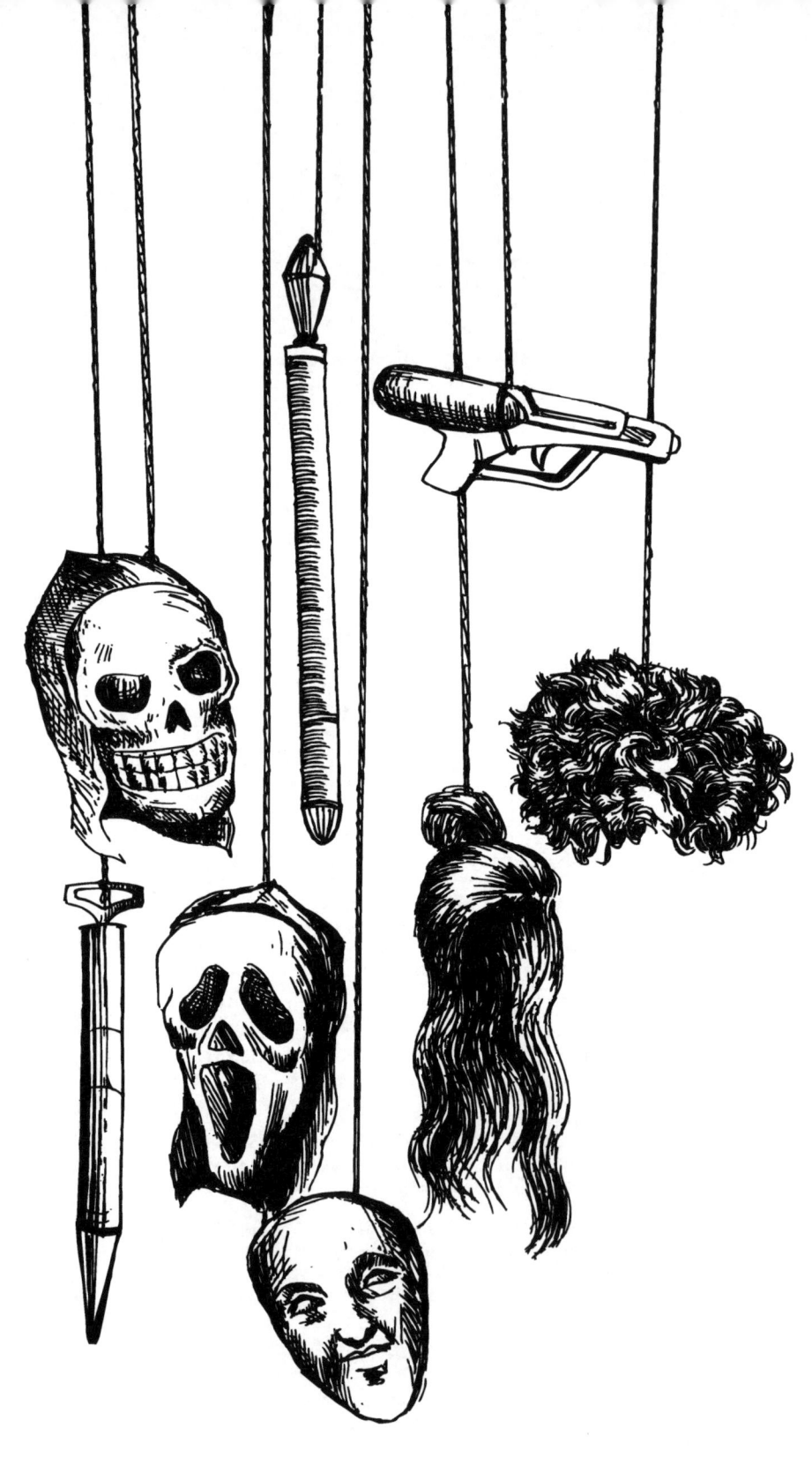

HORROR POEMS

THE HOLLOW PATH

In the hush of dusk, where the wild winds creep,
Through the crooked trees and the bramble's sleep,
Walks a girl in a tattered cloak of black,
With whispers curling down her back.

No name she bears, or none she'll tell,
Her eyes hold storms, her breath a spell.
Crows wheel silent where she treads -
The ground forgets her footprints' threads.

She speaks to shadows, feeds them fire,
Sings in tongues that stir the mire.
The moon, half dead, avoids her gaze,
And stars blink out beneath her haze.

They say she danced with plague and flame,
That wolves once bowed and spoke her name.
A lantern swings from her pale hand -
Its light is cold, not meant for man.

Once, a child chased her through the pine,
Drawn by a voice like shattered wine.
Only bones returned at dawn,
Wrapped in lace and cursed with fawn.

She tends her garden with graveyard soil,
And waters roots with sinner's toil.
Each flower blooms a different face -
All eyes closed, as if in grace.

You may not see her, but she sees you -
In puddles dark or midnight dew.
So, heed this take, and tread with care,
For the girl in the woods is always there.

THE BRIDE BENEATH THE BELFRY

Beneath the bells unholy toll,
A corpse with secrets gnaws its soul.
The bride who died before the dawn,
Now hunts the night – forsaken, drawn.

Her veil, a shroud of writhing night,
Her eyes are pits devoid of light.
Her fingers twist like skeletal snakes,
Her smile – death's cruel masquerade.

The priest's last breath was drowned in sin,
The groom was buried deep within.
Their lives were etched in blood and bone,
Her vow's a curse, eternal, sewn.

She feasts on flesh, the warm, the weak,
Her voice a rasp, a tortured shriek.
Her laughter peals like breaking glass,
A dirge for those who dare to pass.

At midnight, from the grave she claws,
With iron nails and jaws that gnaw.
She drags the cursed to their graves,
To join her in the death she craves.

No mercy waits within her gaze,
No dawn can break her endless haze.
Beware the bells – the bride is near.
To claim the souls, she doomed to sear.

One kiss of cold, one final breath,
And you will drown in living death.
Forever bound in death's cruel tide -
The bride beneath the belfry hides.

THE HOLLOWED WOOD

Beneath a sky of iron grey,
Where moonlight drowns and will not stay,
A forest waits with rooted breath,
Its branches whispering songs of death.

The trees are bones, their bark is scar,
Each knot an unblinking, lidless star.
Their shadows lengthen, clawing deep,
Where secrets coil and nightmares sleep.

The wind laments through hollow veins,
A dirge for blood, a hymn for chains.
No bird dares sing, no creature creeps,
For here the silence always weeps.

At the heart, a clearing black,
A circle where no life comes back.
The soil is rich with nameless pain,
And watered by an endless rain.

Step not within, lest you be claimed,
By roots that hunger, darkly named.
The wood remembers every tread -
And feasts eternal on the dead.

THEY WAIT IN THE WALLS

The house exhales a breath of cold,
And you feel it crawl into your bones.
Footsteps echo where none should tread,
Whispers curl around your bed.

The air is thick with eyes unseen,
Glinting from corners, wet and keen.
Door's slam shut without a hand,
And shadows pool like drowning sand.

They brush your skin with icy grace,
Leave fingerprints no soul should trace.
Your reflection blinks when you do not,
A hollow twin, silent, distraught.

They hum in the walls, in floor, in ceiling,
A chorus of hunger, never healing.
Drawn to your heartbeat, your fleeting breath,
They linger at the border of life and death.

Objects move with cruel intent,
As if the house itself is bent
On teaching fear, on crushing light,
On swallowing warmth in endless night.

You scream – no sound escapes your lips,
They laugh as the candle gutter slips.
Every doorway, every hall, every stair,
Holds their gaze; they are everywhere.

And when you hide, they wait, still near,
Pressing your mind with unbearable fear.
For in this place, the living are prey,
And the dead will never look away

THE HUNGER OF SHADOWS

They gather where the lamplight fades,
In corners carved by darker shades,
Silent watchers, lean and stark,
Feeding on the trembling dark.

They slither long on cobbled stone,
Each one a shape, but not your own,
Their fingers stretch, their faces blur,
They whisper things you never heard.

Behind your step, they always fall,
Yet sometimes one does not at all -
It lingers still when you move on,
A second self, already gone.

Their eyes are void that drink the flame,
Their mouths recite no holy name,
And should you meet their endless stare,
You'll find your soul already there.

For shadows love what light betrays,
They haunt the night, they haunt the days,
And when your body turns to dust,
It's in their arms you'll place your trust

THE ANGEL OF DEATH (FOR THE SINNER)

He waits where the shadows bleed into the floor,
A silent guest at every door.
No trumpet, no hymn, no holy grace -
Just the whisper of bone, the absence of face.

His wings are not feathers but ragged despair,
A tangle of silence, ash, and cold air.
Eyes like voids where the stars are erased,
A hunger unending, a soul never sated.

He does not knock, he does not pray,
He slides through the cracks where the dying lay.
A finger of frost to the heart, to the breath,
The gentle caress of the Angel of Death.

He kisses the lips that are trembling in fear,
Murmurs, "it's time". Our silence is near".
No bargain, no pleading, no desperate cries,
Only the truth in extinguishing eyes.

And yet – behind him, a trail of release,
A merciless mercy, a terrible peace.
For those who have seen him whisper and smile,
Know death walks with beauty – dark and vile.

WHISPERS IN THE WALLS

The house exhales a breath of frost,
Its timbers groan like souls long lost,
A shadow moves where none should tread,
A voice repeats the names of the dead.

The clock strikes one – its hands are wrong,
They tick in whispers, not in song.
A mirror cracks without a touch,
Revealing eyes that know too much.

The floorboards bleed with phantom stains,
They pulse like veins with ghostly pains.
A door once locked swings open wide,
Inviting in what should stay outside.

The night devours the candles' glow,
The windows weep with faces' woe.
And if you listen, still and near,
You'll learn the house has ears to hear.

For the walls remember every scream,
And feasts upon each broken dream.
Step further in – ignore your dread....
This house was built to house the dead.

THE HOUSE THAT WAITS

The house does not just creak at night -
It breaths, it hungers, void of light.
Its walls are damp with something black,
A stench of earth, of graves cracked back.

A child's laugh drips through the air,
Though no one young is living there.
It calls your name in fractured tones,
A choir stitched from marrowed bones.

The wallpaper peels like rotting skin,
Revealing faces pressed within.
Their eyes are wide, their mouths unsealed,
Their screams forever half-concealed.

Your candle dies - the dark takes hold,
The air turns wet; the floor grows cold.
You run, but every door swings shut....
The house has teeth. The house will gut.

And as you pray your soul to keep,
The stairs collapse, the shadows seep.
You realize - far too late to flee -
The house has always lived in thee.

THE GRAVEYARD INSIDE

The yard stretches endless, shadows twist,
Gravestones bow as if to insist.
Each plot a mirror of hollow ache,
Each root a vein that pulls me awake.

The winds drag cries across the clay,
And trees lean close to steal my day.
Bones shift beneath, not still, not cold,
They whisper secrets I cannot hold.

I see your face in every stone,
Yet grasp at nothing, I am alone.
The soil moves like a breathing heart,
It swallows pieces of me apart.

Branches scratch like fingernails,
And darkness hums with ghostly wails.
The graveyard pulses with grief's own blood,
Rivers of sorrow, thick as mud.

I walk its paths, yet cannot leave,
Your absence blooms; it will not grieve.
The earth, the stones, the air – they know,
And in their arms, my soul lies low.

The yard is alive, it whispers, it sees,
It keeps my heart; it never frees.
Each step I take, each shuddered breath,
Is caught and held by endless death.

THE CHILD BENEATH MY SLEEP

She crawls from cracks where daylight dies,
A little girl with rotting eyes.
Her teeth are black, her whispers red,
She asks for help among the dead.

Her nails scrape bone inside my head,
She pulls me closer to her bed
Of dirt and worms, of roots and rain,
A coffin stitched with children's pain.

I do not know the thing she seeks,
Her voice is blood that stains my cheeks.
Her mouth is wide, it eats my breath,
Her fingers smell of mold and death.

She will not leave, she will not rest,
Her cries are knives against my chest.
And every night her shadows creep -
The child who feeds beneath my sleep.

Scots Poems

MA FIFER LASS

She's fire – raw, unchained,
Walks in a room and the Deil himsel' steps back,
Aye, step back,
Cos, he kens she'll burn his pride,
Burn it clean, leive nae ash behinde.

She's thistle an' steel,
Staunch as the stane,
Timper like a storm,
Hert like the Tay-deep, wild, relentless.

She speaks, the hills ken hur voice,
The sea whispers hur name,
Nae hush can haud hur,
Nae shadow can hide hur.

She's a Fifer,
Blood hot, mind shairp,
Feet firme, nieve ridy,
Luv bigger'n hur hert can haud.

She fichts, she luvs,
She lauchs, she storms,
She's Scotland it a peek,
Freedom in a braith.

And if ye hink ye kin brek hur,
Hink againe.
Ma lass disnae brek.
Ma lass disnae ben.
Ma lass – she burns!

A FAITHER'S PRIDE

Fower bonnie lassies, braw an' braw,
Ilk ane a licht, a sicht tae awe.
Frae eldest tae the youngest wee,
They fill ma hert wi' boundless glee.

Thair lauchter rings, thair courage glows,
In ilka step, ma spirit knows:
The world may try tae bend, tae sway,
Bit ma dochters shine, com whit may.

Thair minds sae kenn, thair herts sae true,
They cirry wisdom, kindness too.
Ilka day a watch thaim tak' tae flight,
An' swell wi' pride baith day an' nicht.

Tho storms may com, an' lifts grow grey,
Thair luve, thair strength, lichts up ma day.
Wi' fower bricht stars guidin' oor hame,
A Faither's pride will aye remain.

LIFT YER HEID, LASSIE

Lift yer heid, lassie, the dawn is bricht,
The hills are dancin' in morning licht.
The haar has lifted, the path is clear,
Tak a brave wee step, ye've nowt tae fear.

The thistle blooms where the winds hae cried,
Strong and wild by the riverside.
It daurs tae grow whaur nane would try-
So can you, wi' heart held high.

Though storms may batter, though rain may fa'
Yer spirit's made o' highland braw.
Ye're forged in fire, in kin and glen,
Stronger still than ye'll ever ken.

Sangs o' old still ride the breeze,
Through ancient stones and whisperin' trees.
They tell ye this: ye're no alone-
This land, this sky, they mark ye grown.

So stravaig on, wi' soul sae wide,
Let hope and pride walk by yer side.
For every burn, and brae, and ben
Is singin' aye, "Rise up again!"

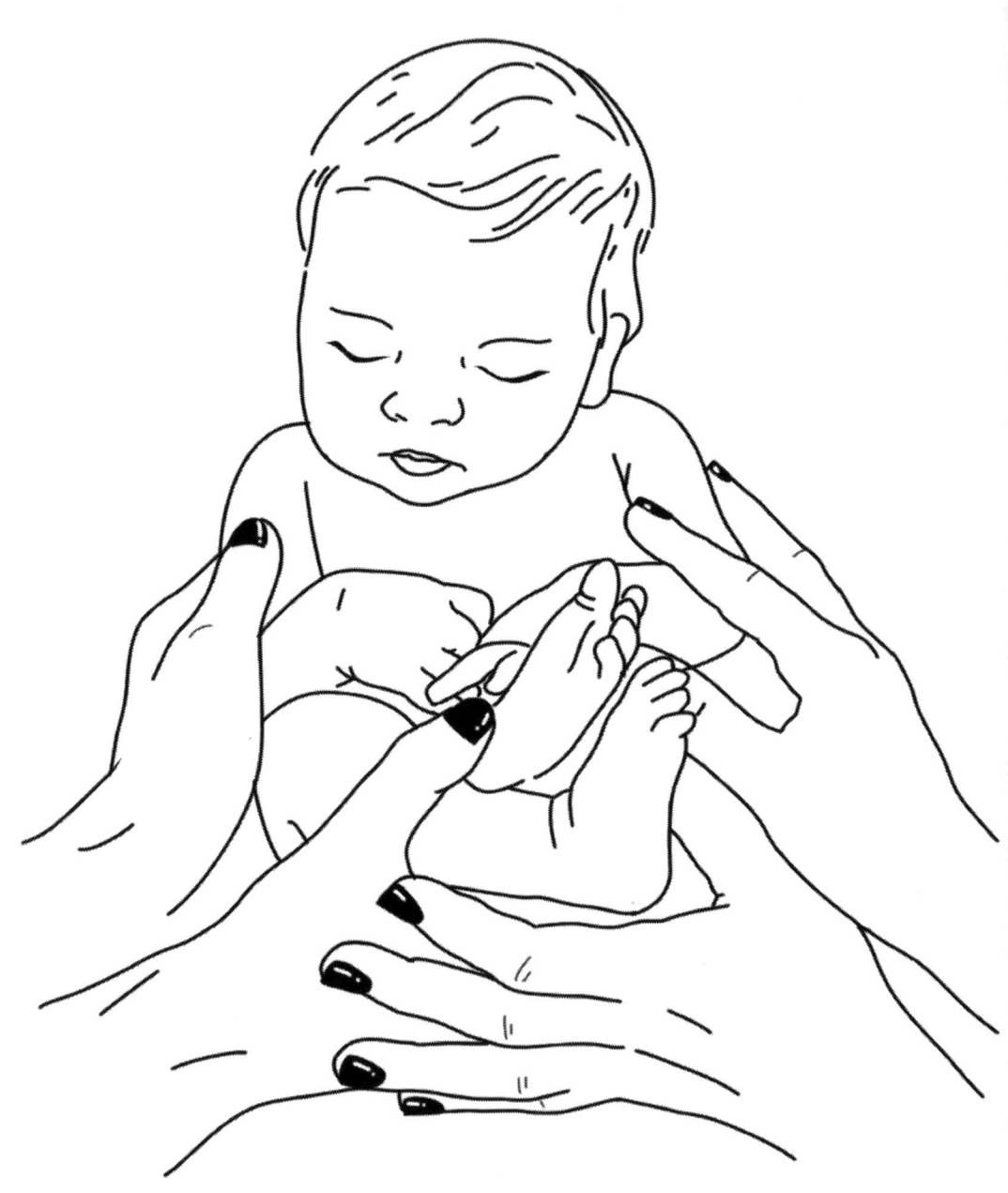

A NEW BAIRN

The nicht wis stil' and quiet,
Ten cam yer very first greet,
A soon sae sweet, sae tender,
It lifted herts on high.

Yer face sae pink an' bonnie,
Wee fingers curled in haun,
Ye've brocht a glo o' wonner,
Like sunrise ower the lan'!

Yer mammy's een are glistening,
Yer daddy's fair in awe,
The hoose is fu' o' happiness,
Nae joy like this wi' saw.

O bairn, yer oor blessin',
Oor hope, oor licht, oor song,
Frae this day forth, we'll guide yi,
An' luve yi a' life long.

WEE REID-HEIDED LASSIE

She struts doon the street
Hoodie up, curls burstin oot
Like sparks frae a firework
Nae chance O blendin in.

Aye folk stare
But she jist gies thum tha' smirk
The yin tha' says
"Try me, if yer daft enough".

Thurs steel in hur step
Bit kindness hingin at the edges
A hert big as the Forth
An stubborn as ony tide.

Ma wee reid-heided lassie
Blazin hur ain road
Nae dimmer switch built
Fir a soul tha' birns this bricht.

A WEE BIT BANTER ABOOT SCOTLAND

Scotland's cauld, aye, that's nae lie,
Ye'll freeze yer neb if ye gang oot dry.
But gie us rain, or snaw, or mist,
We'll still cry, "aye, this land is bliss!".

The midgies bite, the wind blaws sair,
Yer brolly turns tae scrap oot there.
Yit in the pub, wi' pint in haun,
Ye'll aye feel warm across the lan'.

Frae tattie scones tae haggis neat,
Wi' Irn-Bru tae keep ye sweet,
Wi' ceilidh steps an' heid fu' sang,
Ye'll ken ye've bided here ower lang.

So, raise yer dram, ye sons an' dochters,
Frae Hebridean isles tae Borders -
Fir a' oor flaws, we're staunch an' kind,
Na better folk ye're like tae find.

THE PIPER O GLENCOE

Listen.

The glen disnea sleep.
The glen niver sleeps.

It hauds the soond-
Pipes risin', rowin,
Like thunner blawn frae breath,
Like a hertbeat carved in stane.

This isnea greetin.
This isnea silence.
This is fire through the mist,
A voice aulder'n war,
Aulder'n dule,
Greetin we're still here.

The piper stauns,
An the bens staun wi him.
Ilk note climbs the brae,
Loup the burn,
Strikes yer breist like a drum.

He blaws fir the clans,
Fir the bairns that lauch in the heather,
For ilk step that daurs the heich road.
He blaws fir the leevin,
An the deid rise tae dance.

Glencoe answers-
Stane tae sky-
Sky tae sang,
Sang tae fowk.

An the promise roars back:
We'll no vanish,
We'll no bow.
Thair'll aye be music,
Aye be pride,
Aye be Glencoe.

A DREAM O' ALBA

O Scotland, bonnie, free an' braw,
Wi' hills tha' rise an' lochs tha' ca',
Yer heather glows in purple sheen,
A lan' sae prood, sae fierce, sae keen.

Frae Wallace' Claymore, tae freedom's flame,
Nae tyrant's yolk shall dim oor name,
His courage roars through glen an' glade.
A hero's spirit ne'er tae fade.

The win' blaws through the ancient braes,
Wi' tale o' clans, o' heroes' days,
Nae foreign haun, nae cruel plan,
Can bind the hert o' this brave lan'.

So, raise yer banners, tartan braw,
Fir Alba's sons an' dochters a',
Wi' Wallace' spirit, prood an' auld,
Wi'll hae oor freedom, strang an' bauld.

ALBA'S DAY

Nae mair tae ben', nae chains tae bare,
Scotland rises wi' win-blawn hair,
The north win' sings, the hills reply,
Oor lan' is free, oor spirits high.

Frae Borders south tae Hebrideas' shore,
Nae English haun shall rule us o'er,
Oor thistle's bloom, oor banners fly,
Wi' tartan pride an' steely ee.

The ghosts O' Wallace, Bruce, an Knox
Stride wi us noo, unlockin' locks,
Oor voice is loud, oor herts are braw,
Alba staunds free, nae England's law.

Sae raise yer pipes, yer drums, yer song,
The time o' chains is deed an' gone,
Oor lan', oor kin, oor hame sae dear,
Staunds free at las', wi' nane tae fear.

BRAES DIVIDED

Aneath the heather, braid an'wild,
A MacLean lass met MacDonalds son.
Thair een did meet, thair herts did yearn,
Yit warldly feud sade "nae concern".

Frae rival clans, oor bairns wir torn,
Wi' whispered vows in gloamin' born.
The glens rang low wi' secret lauch,
Yit danger staket the braes sae rough.

Thair luve wis fire, sae fierce, sae sweet,
A dance o' herts nae feud could beat.
Bit clans wi' pride, wi' Claymores held high,
Saw nane bit traitors 'neath the sky.

Oor lovers met where rivers braid,
In hidden groves, in moonlit glade.
Thair herts entwined, thair spirits braw,
A love forbidden, aye still law.

Though clans migh' fight an' elders froon,
Nae wa', nae Claymore can keep thum doon.
Fir luve, it blooms, sae bold, sae free,
A MacLean lass, a MacDonald he.

About the Author

Vicky Donald, known to many as Vix, is a poet from Fife, Scotland. Her debut collection, Beneath the Thistle Sky, is a heartfelt reflection on love, loss, family, and the beauty that can be found in both strength and vulnerability.

Vix discovered her love for words through her Grandad, who nurtured her imagination and passion for storytelling. Years later, her S4 English teacher, Mr. Boyd, reignited that creative spark and reminded her that her voice had meaning.

Now a proud wife and mother of four daughters, Vix draws inspiration from the everyday moments that shape her — the laughter, the lessons, and the lasting bonds of family. Her poetry carries pieces of the people she loves, the memories she treasures, and the Scottish landscape that surrounds her.

Beneath the Thistle Sky is both a tribute and an invitation — a glimpse into a life lived with open eyes and an open heart.

Printed in Great Britain
by Amazon

fc69df1a-8ede-49a3-ba1e-d3bea632e6b5R01